The BOX

**By Madeline Boskey
Illustrated by Jeff Hopkins**

Target Skill Plot

Scott Foresman
is an imprint of

PEARSON

Glenview, Illinois • Boston, Massachusetts • Chandler, Arizona •
Upper Saddle River, New Jersey

Mom gave Kim a big box.
"Have fun," said Mom.

"I can make a home!" said Kim.
"Will you cut this, Mom?" Kim said.

Meg said, "I have rugs."
Kim said, "Those rugs can go in here."

Bud said, "I have a big cat."
Kim said, "That big cat can go in here."

Max said, "I have nice snacks."
Kim said, "Those nice snacks can go in here."

Nan said, "I have five red cups."
Kim said, "Those five red cups can go in here."

We had fun.
We made a fine home for us!